The Woman Who Knew

poems by

Donna Aza

Finishing Line Press
Georgetown, Kentucky

The Woman Who Knew

There are many kinds of open
how a diamond comes into a knot of flame
how sound comes into a word, coloured
by who pays what for speaking.

from "Coal" by Audre Lorde

...wondering
which me will survive all these liberations.

from "Who Said It Was Simple" by Audre Lorde

Editor: Christen Kincaid

Cover Art: Jedhi Weir

Author Photo: Lifetouch Portrait Studios, Inc.

Cover Design: Elizabeth Maines

Printed in the USA on acid-free paper.
Order online: www.finishinglinepress.com
also available on amazon.com

Author inquiries and mail orders:
Finishing Line Press
P. O. Box 1626
Georgetown, Kentucky 40324
U. S. A.

Table of Contents

A Kind of Paradise

That night
we bathed together
in Bois Content
from one large aluminum pan
used for scrubbing clothes
in an outdoor bathroom
made of unpainted concrete blocks
rubbing our feet smooth
on the rough concrete floor
splashing cold rain water on each other
and shivering, and you wrapped me
in the oversized beach towel and ran
naked into the house yourself—whooping—
it was the best sleep we ever had.

Early in the morning Ralph came
with a handful of the good stuff
from his field— and I looked
the other way.

—You said my home was a kind of paradise—.

The next day
we drove to the prophet parish
and sat with your mother
who looks like Cedella,
then took the hills to Nine Miles
to pay our respects to Bob
and you chastised the kids
singing Redemption Song
and hustling us by the gate.

Our sons caught a poltergeist
on camera at Garvey's house
after the tenant tried to charge us
US $50 to look inside.

We passed Burning Spear's place
but could not see beyond the wall
and ended up—
where we always end up.

At Dunn's River
we climbed the waterfall,
you holding my hand.
That day I did not slip.

Five of us—huddled together—under the heaviest deluge.

Making Room for Family

We always liked having guests, even the house liked visitors.
You could feel it expanding to make room, could almost hear it exhale.

The first time D came we spread the quilt under the almond tree
And though only a few yards from the house, we put ice in the cooler.

With grapes, cheese, crackers, watermelon, and white wine for the grownups
and just lay out in the sun, all five of us (we were a family of four then).

Nibbling and shooting the breeze. Lizards skittered by in the grass,
a moth landed on my arm, someone was riding a jet ski in the canal

      —but that was all that broke the calm—.

That day I wrote a poem about children chasing butterflies
You made us curried tofu with hot peppers and coconut milk for dinner.

D talked about the gay pride parade in New York
I watched your eyes, but they gave nothing away.

No fire and brimstone, no talk of Sodom and Gomorrah
No burning of Babylon, just an irie vibe, spicy vegan food.

A few laughs and a heart as open as our home
That day I decided to stay⌐—a little longer.

The Woman Who Knew

He's so good with baby birds, I had said.
He's always rescuing them
and feeding them till they grow quite big
and are so tame they never fly away.

Well, you're not a baby bird, are you? she said
sucking her teeth.

Dwayne and Molina

They were siblings—
one white with black markings   one gray   a boy and a girl.
They climbed the sofa, chewed my slipper, made the nanny nervous,
would not stay outside. The kids fed them milk from the baby's old bottle.

Claremont came to dinner—
saw the pen out back and laughed. "Y'all tink yuh back home?"
Better than dogs, you said. All they eat is grass—goat shit don't stink.
The boys loved them, though they wanted a dog. Miss D pursed her lips.

In beautiful San Andres—
I read my paper, sat by the pool, took a boat to an almost deserted island
where I met a dog, Lamb's Bread, and his owner, and danced
to a Mento band, great-grandchildren of Jamaican immigrants.

I called home—
to tell you about the Jamaican-Columbians, fighting for their freedom.
The kids came on, each one in turn, then you. All's well, you said.
Miss Doris came on. We have no milk, she said. Hurry home.

Your husband went to the store—
He bought milk for the goats, none for the baby. I told my sister-friend.
She burst out laughing. So I laughed too, which was a bad idea. I fell
into a laughing fit. I laughed till my belly cramped, till my sides ached.

Royal Poinciana

Some days she does not endure.
There are hours that beat and she breaks
 things   shatters worlds
—but she is anything but a bore—.

She's a conjure woman
mother   teacher   wildspiritwoman
midwife of words and a harlot   some nights
an ole hige flying skinless through the trees.

Kiss of wind—sliver of rain
dancing silver moonbeam.

—She's a trick and a tease—
a warm breath in your ear
a three minute grind in a smoky club
a sip of over-proof white rum—a scarlet secret
a bright blue feather falling
the blood-shot eye of a hurricane
a devastating earthquake
a vulture
a screech owl
an ancient tree spirit
a forest of yellow snakes
moldy tree bark and sticky black-tar molasses
sour gum and sweet william
an ache in middle-aged loins
a sweet caress, a shout, a whisper
an old fire stick bursting into flames.

A bright red glowing
in the dark green forest of you.

Like Water in a Basket

I knew your silence would stain these walls one day, and
yet I carried on loving you.

I threw my laughter into the wind, now I hear the muted
echo of an empty well.

The water you gave me to carry trickles from the basket
you gave me to carry it in.

I'll poke bigger holes in the straw-setting, let it gush out,
wash my face clean.

My Soul Wakes Up

Sunlight glitters like molten gold
on the green, green leaves.

The earth turns over in her sleep
and I slowly wake up from a dream
threatening to pilfer my body
and purloin my soul.

When You See It Coming

Come with me to hear this poet sing, I had begged—ten years ago.
"No, you go if you want to. I'm not in the mood." My husband said.

I got dressed: floral maxi skirt, bright orange halter top, black high heels.
I was looking damn hot. Fabulous and a few years short of forty.

My sistren came to pick me up, locks hanging down her petite bare back.
We went to the club to hear the poet chant—two fine women in our prime.

Place was jam-packed. The DJ played: "Mama Africa."
Feeling royal, we danced, laughed, had two drinks. Poet took the stage.

He electrified the place—lifted us higher. When we came down I ran
Home—to tell my man about the poet who had renewed my faith.

The house was clamoring with a rage—only I could hear.
But you sure could feel the cold, sharp wind of a fight brewing.

I placed the CD into his hands and watched as it danced across the room.
It smashed against the edge of the entertainment center—and cracked.

Like a life cracks   years before splintering   into pieces.

A Matter of Life

You're so lucky
(the church women say)
Your husband is always home.

My husband is always home
has no friends, goes to work
eats dinner in front of the tv.

My husband brings home his pay
Sneaks beer when I go to bed
Can't do anything fun without me.

My husband does not give to charity
likes his world to fit in the living room.
People who don't know say—

My husband is a good man.
My husband believes friendship between
a man and a woman is a prelude to sex.

I have friendships with men
(at cafes, farmers' markets, libraries)
that lead to coffee, vegan recipes, poetry.

My husband does not read poetry—
is a master jeweler—his teacher told me.
My husband does not make jewelry.

My husband is a talented artist
He paints half-heartedly
One oil every five years.

My husband does not pay bills
buy groceries or talk
He will mow the lawn if I nag.

My husband does not correct
his sons, go to their games, or teach
them about puberty or dating.

He grunts when they speak to him
shifts position in his chair
waves them away with one hand.

My husband is barely alive (unless angry)
He sleeps on the recliner
One eye open—tv watching him.

I must leave my husband
So he can resurrect
He will hate me for eternity

—a small price.

Until Good Advice
(For Loris)

For the people who ask "why did you stay so long?"
You should ask them: "Is a marriage something you're supposed to leave
after the first fight—the second—the tenth?"

If not after the first thru the tenth, then after how many quarrels
do you leave a marriage? What is the perfect, politically correct
number of fights after which you ought to walk away?

After you say until death do you part, do you then say:
Until the first sign of jealousy, until he loses his job, his temper?
Until he accuses you of thinking you're smarter than him?

Do you stay until he refuses to feed the kids while you're at work?
Or until you suspect he's the one having an affair—because
he acts jealous of everyone, including your students?

Do you leave after you have an emotional affair? (which is always worse)
Or after he wrestles you to the floor and takes your phone all day
to see if your pretend lover will call?

And since you're wrong, and since you're not sure if wrestling is hitting
do you call the Popo on your husband? Even more scary—
So what if you decide to run to your friend instead and he follows?

And what if your friend says: "You can spend one night,
but my husband is not here and I am afraid. You don't have to go home,
but you can't stay here." What if you feel embarrassed?

What if you get up early to go looking at apartments
and then you remember your mortgage is in your name. Out of spite,
he will not pay it. What if you can't afford a mortgage and rent?

Your kids will be back from vacation soon and damn it you need a plan.

And what if your friend says: "Shouldn't you be thinking job security?
Book & tenure first, divorce later." *(Now, why didn't you think of that?)*

Then your sister says the same thing—laying it out like a blueprint:
"We spend years planning our wedding, why not plan our divorce?"

You open a separate account—and begin working out your exit strategy.

Buddha Belly

I'm watching my body
pad itself in protective folds
rounding out preemptively
in preparation for the blow.

It is a miracle I tell you
these round melons of breasts
and strong jackfruit thighs
armoring up to fight for me.

Buddha belly smiling up at me, holy
backside defying gravity and fate.

My body is laughing at life, teasing
beckoning to the schoolyard bully:

"Come on, come nuh.   We ready fi yuh."

What They Don't Tell You
(For H.R.)

They say some women like to call the police and lie about abuse—
They don't tell you that for some women the police show up too late.

They say that your lawyer cannot use the testimony of your friends—
They don't tell you that your lawyer might find you too strong to be credible.

They say that he may harass you; his lawyer will try to intimidate you—
They don't tell you his lawyer will bully a judge/get her recused for bias.

They say that a female judge might be more inclined to believe you—
*They don't tell you that she may say there's no **imminent** danger:*

—"It has been four months since the last incident."—

They say that some of your mutual friends will defect to his side—
They don't tell you that some, who didn't like him, will desert you.

They say that you will really learn who your true friends are—
They don't tell you that your ride or die will show up in court to testify.

They say your lawyer will protect your interests if you pay him well—
They don't tell you that only works for housewives with rich spouses.

They say he will have to pay child support, because it's mandatory—
*They don't tell you that if you have a **good** job, you may end up paying him.*

They say he can only get out of child support if he's time-sharing—
They don't tell you that enforcing it, is time & money wasted.

They say if you're a strong woman you should just keep fighting—
They don't tell you the toll it takes on your kids, your health & work.

They say you will have moments of regret/death by misogynoir—
They don't tell you you'll wake up, peace in the house, & feel only relief.

Loved to Pieces

I like the purple shirt   you wore to court today
& your new black fedora   was very becoming
I didn't like the dyed beard   the extensions
like lies   covering the bald spots.

Duplicity   exposed to light
so the world   can see
what I already   know
neither righteous   nor royal.

Not a lion   of the tribe of judah
not a defender   of the pride
an erstwhile   gold-smith/artist
turned   gold-digger.

Ready to mine   your own children
from their home   for a price
a back   &   belly rat
scavenging   for cheese.

Ego   &   jealousy
Fear   &   insecurity
Gnawing away   at our delicate cover
exposing us   to the elements.

To damp   &   mold
for years I tried   to lullaby it
to rock   &   church
& patch the coldness   into peace.

Too many years   I tried to save us
for what we were   and could have been
tacking new squares   onto the rat-bitten quilt
but the dry-rot   had already set in.

Every stitch   ripped another gash
into our family   a toxic & paralyzing fear
ruptured   the weakest thread
love worn thin   till there was no backing left

              to-bind-the-pieces-together.

Eating Grief

Two sunny sides down
eighteen years and three children
Two smirking fat cats.

Ras Levi Speaks

It was her first time going up to Red Hills
I took her to meet my elder and his tribe
seven little Rasta princes and princesses
no mothers—Just Ras Levi and his youth.

Me and the elder sitting on the back verandah
looking down on Kingston
I and I, sons of Nyahbinghi
deep in reasoning
holding a sacrament
tuning the drum.

                    —Ras Levi turned to me—
*So, I see the I in love (he sucks deep, blows out smoke) but I going show the I something.
I know the I not going to like what I have to say. But so I see it, so I sell it. This woman
is not for the I, seen? This woman is of the world. It's not going to work. This woman is
too independent, too educated, full of self. This woman spell trouble. This woman dress
like the world. Talk like a book. And look me in the eye like a man. This woman will
never know her place. She will never let you wear the pants. I'm not saying she is Jezebel
or Delilah. That is for you to know for yourself, but this woman is not humble enough.
She think she is as good as any man.*

I was a Kushite
I knew this was false teachings
What about Queen Nyahbinghi?

                    But I looked up to Ras Levi.

A meditation dropped heavy in my heart
something soft in me hardened
that night I picked a fight with her
I kept it up, on and off, until we left the island.

She kept asking what had gotten into me
I couldn't tell her

I made love to her until she forgot
what a bastard I had been
until she forgave me.

                    Fuck Ras Levi. I was happy.

When we returned to California
I asked her to marry me
I could not believe she said yes.
I told myself—

>   Ras Levi was
>   Jealous
>   Bitter
>   Lonely
>   A false prophet.

I was the true Nyahbinghi   I could handle a strong Queen.

I Asked Jah for Her

I requested her—
A conscious woman is a rare find. But a pretty Jamaican
graduate student? Only Jah!

I admired her—
She was different. Independent. Rootsy. Feisty.
Raising her son alone.

I courted her—
I replaced her tiles and carpet. Nights—she tutored athletes.
I waited at the bus stop.

I taught her—
To cook vegan, to drive, and that a man could be counted on.
I became her best friend.

I married her—
It was simple. We loved each other. We planned to do it big—later.
She didn't mind.

I painted her—
After she had my son, she was something. Pretty eyes, lavish hair
skin like sapodilla.

I accused her—
Once bitten—I swear no woman would ever cheat on me again.
No male "friends."

I levelled her—
Sometimes I had to check her. A doctorate doesn't make you
better than anyone.

I backed her—
She landed the job. We bought a house. I painted Maroon Nanny
to fight for us.

I followed her—
From West to South. I lost—friends—the business we had
built together.

I controlled her—
We fought. I cultivated silence. I barred the door. I hid her keys.
I stopped painting.

I ran her—
I couldn't tell you the exact moment I checked out.
Soon—only my body was there.

I lost her—
She served me papers. I begged—on my knees. I cried.
She slept.

Haiku for Lost Love

"Black love is a revolutionary act." —Dr. Frances Welsing

I'm mad as hell too
I know what we could have been
Good Black love—with wings.

I Almost Called Today

Not one call returned in seventeen months
Still, I almost called today.
You see I found an injured bird today
—and though you did not respond to middle son—
on crutches, taking the car and getting 4 tickets
losing his natural mind—over losing you
I thought you might respond to a bird that fell out of its nest.

Who knows better than you how to care for an injured winged thing?
How to keep it warm, chew up its food
feed it from your mouth, and fret over it like a mother
bird   until the day its feathers grow in.

Then who knows better than you how to clip those wings
how to make of your hand a branch for it to sit on
kiss its pointy beak and prune its short tail feathers
tame it so well it follows you around like you're its mother
and never ever wants to leave its cage.

Who knows better than you how to line the bars with shiny things
with baubles and colorful seeds—how to turn a finch into a magpie.
How to take your winged thing on nature hikes

to watch fledglings fall—
                              and
                              learn
                              fear
                              of
                              flying.

Safe

The hole you punched in the door
is patched over spackled and painted
a different tone of white than the white noise
in my bedroom as the morning light
streams in at 7 am.

My window is open.
I can hear birds singing
One   two three   six
different sounds six different birds?
or is it one bird in six different
cadences I can never tell.

—The noise beneath the quiet—

A low humming sound
rising from the earth
bees   & other winged
things buzzing
the distant sound
of a lawn mower
a plane flying overhead
my neighbor starting his car
my heart beating.

—Sky opens without warning—

Rain falls in one long sheet
drowning all other sounds
I fixed the roof
did you know that?
rain no longer falls
through the cracks.

I snuggle under the covers
still sticking to my side
of the bed I stretch
my hand across
the emptiness on your side

—and breathe a prayer of thanks—.

A Clear Window of Glass

First thing—
Remove the ugly, peeling-away, dark tint from the solid glass window.

Then—
Take down the faded blinds— older than my ten year old and falling apart.

At last—
I have my window clear to see the trees outside: almond, mango, pear.

I can see clear—
all the way to the canal. I can't see the water, but I know it is there waiting.

I split the family—
room in two. Now for each child, a room of his own, his own mess.

Each can mourn—
in private. Hate me. Scream at the walls painted in his favorite colors.

What should I do—
now, except worry about the kids, the bills? I clean, cry, Facebook.

Finally—
I place my desk by the wall of glass and write all the green I see.

Sister Mary
(for Tracy)

I got off light—the righteous women say.
On my block alone two wives wash, feed and comb
the hair of their husband's little indiscretions
—young enough to be their grandchildren.

Church women fare the worst.
There's always a bible verse
to justify the bit
in a woman's mouth.

Sister Jones wanted to adopt the child
Deacon Jones brought home.
Instead she lost deacon
and not even to the child's mother.

Jesus-women—blessed art thou
more weight on the cross you bear
—closer to the kingdom
Sister Mary was not so lucky.

The bank took the house
while her husband took the car
leaving the Saint-in-Christ
to take the bus—in sun or rain.

With two young sons
to church and school
soccer practice   , piano lessons
gymnastics and Spanish classes.

At the library on Saturdays
Sister Mary is determined
her boys will be somebodies
someday—no matter the cost.

But those clever boys
are not too cultured
to smell new poop
to shake the pink rattle.

One night I dreamed
about Mary and woke up
quoting scripture
I saw a petite woman.

Flying across the room
propelled by a muscular arm
with a doctor bird tattoo
like the one on her husband.

The devil already hated me
for man-handling my poor husband
out of the house—for how else
did I get a king to leave his castle?

I told Mary the dream
but she was not ready to leave
having no place to go
with two kids—that I understood.

So I told Mary: "mi casa es su casa."
Until you are ready to leave
remember what the good book says:
"a soft answer turneth away wrath"

—and if that don't work call me—.

Coffee with Mary

For me, therefore, trust is a deep knowing that all is well. It is a deep and abiding belief in the orderliness of the Universe – despite "evidence" to the contrary."
Marguerite Orane, Free and Laughing.

Look at you—free and
laughing with a fading mark
on your ring finger.

Looking at Pictures of Yosemite

I am glad you made us buy that disposable panoramic camera
The view is every bit as stunning as I remember—
I still study the pictures. For a cheap camera, they have held up
pretty good. Against the backdrop of majestic granite cliffs
domes, spires, and trees as thick as thieves and as old as California,
and more beautiful, stands our little family.

Son-1
is baked mahogany brown and shirtless
wearing his green sweat pants and carrying a stick.
Son-2
is walking with my friend, June
carrying the ropes for climbing.
The baby-
is being pushed in his blue & red umbrella stroller
by
Ms. Doris-
who is wearing a floral dress
and shoes that are not for hiking.
My hair-
is in twists and I am way more slender
than I am now. Slimmer than I remember ever being
in my adult life—with kids.
There is a reddish glow about my face and head
as if the sun was setting when the picture was taken.
I am the only one frowning, mouth open,
like I was saying something urgent
as the picture was snapped.

You are not in the picture
so you must have been taking it.
Nothing of terror shows in the picture,
so I don't know if it was taken before or after that fight.
Before or after the ride along the precipitous road,
the car barely clinging to the cliff side.
You were at the wheel and we were having an argument
which quickly turned nasty.
We hurtled along the cliff,
every second a second away from certain death.
I cannot remember what provoked the fight,
so I don't know who was wrong,
but I must have thought I was right
because at first I argued ardently

like I argue when I think I am right.
It is a Libra curse—one of our many contradictions.
We hate conflict, but will duel to the death
to get to our precious peace.
So I must have been feeling righteous
because I was definitely not dropping it,
which must mean it was half my fault—
it takes two, right?
I stopped arguing when you sped up
along the winding road   edging
those steep Yosemite cliffs. If the car fell over
the cliff it would be a long drop down
the craggy mountainside
to the icy lake
at the base
to smash through
straight into that ethereal
lake of glass
where we would surely freeze
to death
if we made it down
alive.
But we would never make it in one piece.
The car would be twisted
like a pretzel
on those majestic
mountains.
All my bones would be crushed to pieces
and there would be nothing left of me
to bury.

I must have been feeling paper thin
and very insubstantial
because I distinctly remember thinking
I would be crushed to a bloody mush
if we fell
so many hundreds of feet
to the bottom of the cliff,
into the dark green valley below,
probably into El Capitan
picnic area, scarring
somebody's children for life.

Later, you would say—
you were only trying to scare me into shutting up.
Of course, you would never crash the car and kill yourself
(along with me). Well, you succeeded in scaring
the sass out of me. I got quiet and calm, real quick:
"Alright, I am sorry. Forget the argument.
Please slow down, babe, you win."
I remember whispering just loud enough for you to hear,
scared for real now, my breath coming shallow and raspy.
I no longer cared who was right.
I just wanted to steer you and the car
away from the cliff-side.

I thought about my children
growing up without me,
but I am almost ashamed to admit
that what scared me the most
was the thought that other than
a Ph.D.,
a mortgage,
a student loan
and three kids—
I had no legacy to leave behind.

I had a few poems in academic journals
one short story in an anthology
one personal essay
in a second rate magazine
a raggedy bunch
of unpublished poems
on my hard drive
and my half-finished memoir.

My life as a writer did not amount to much.
Some of my students would miss me and maybe my mother
would keen like an ole African at a funeral,
and although you'd already be dead
she would most certainly
curse the day you were born
(without even knowing you were at fault)
and trace every generation in your family tree.
My sister would hate you with an eternal
silent hatred—as only she can.

My boys would be pathetic orphans
—that thought was unbearable,
but not nearly as unbearable
as the thought of dying
without publishing even one book,
and maybe that would be no great loss to the world,
maybe my poems would speak to no one but me,
but the thought of never finding out was
heartbreaking.

People would say—
"So much potential, such a waste of a life…"
(admittedly, it wasn't much of a life yet, but who knew?)
What if I had greatness inside of me?
You mean no one (meaning me) would ever find out?

I touched your hand again,
ever so lightly, my eyes pleading.
You mouthed something that I could not hear
and flashed my hand off your arm
without cutting your speed.
I had no seat belt on and struggled
to get it fastened as I flew forward
into the dashboard of the rented SUV.

We hurtled wildly around razor sharp turn
after razor sharp turn,
the beauty of the place made more surreal
when seen like an old movie reel in fast forward—
flashes of icy peaks,
majestic trees rushing by,
the unearthly quality of the light
right before the sun set.
It was like being in a tilt-a-whirl at Disney World,
but instead of brightly painted fairytale buildings
it was spectacular trees and enchanted ice caps
flashing by so fast I was getting vertigo.
The blood was pumping in my head,
the river in my ears was thrashing wildly,
crashing against even wilder thoughts,
and I could see your jaws working furiously
and the veins in your neck popping out.

My whole life did not flash before my eyes,
but the events of the last few idyllic days did flow
across the screen—
the early morning hike through Yosemite valley to the river,
you dipping the baby in the legendary cold water of the Merced,
how he had gasped in surprise and then began laughing hysterically.
And I thought, of the three kids, maybe he alone would be ok
without us, even at the tender age of two and a half.
But, mostly, I remember thinking:
how incredibly beautiful the cliffs were
and the valley below, so green,
and how the climb the morning before to Vernal Falls
had been worth the two hours it took us to get there
because of the wild flowers
and squirrels on the trail,
one of which the boys chased up a tree,
the family of deer we ran into
as we turned the bend in the trail
after leaving the camping shop
(made to look like it was an organic
part of the valley with its natural wood and rustic design),
and meeting the Guyanese family from San Francisco
and exchanging numbers and promises,
the spectacular view of the fall
when we got to the top of the trail
and, above all, that glorious rainbow
arching across the base of the water-fall.
It was awesome—
just as holy as it had been the first time
we came to Yosemite on a camping trip
when we were dating,
and saw God in the rainbow.
And told ourselves it was a sign
we should get married.

How proud I had been of you then
for being such an expert camper,
for knowing how to put up a tent in record time,
being able to make a fire much faster
than the seasoned campers we had met on the trail
who were constantly doling out unsolicited advice
(apparently they didn't know we Jamaicans
have common sense and do everything Bolt fast),

and knowing what to do to keep the bears away from me,
—I was precious to you then—.

And you had called me beautiful,
even after three days of camping and no make-up.
And no mirror to see myself in, but your eyes.
And only quick showers, and my braids getting fuzzy.
You had kept holding my chin up to that magical light
—I have only ever seen in Yosemite—
and saying how you wished you had brought your sketch-pad
so you could draw my almond-shaped brown eyes.

And now here you were trying to drive me off a cliff.
We were going to die in one of the most beautiful places
in the world, certainly the most beautiful place
we had ever been together, at that point
and it was not at all romantic.
Worst of all, no one would ever know it was not an accident.
You kept shaking my hand off your arm,
and instinctively I knew if I shouted back,
or made a wrong move, we would both be dead
in a heap at the bottom of the cliff.
So I kept touching your arm very lightly,
speaking only with my hand on your skin
(and even then I thought your skin felt smooth,
and cool to my touch, and your deeply brown skin
looked golden-brown in that light,
and maybe I would be seeing and feeling
your pretty skin for the last time).

I kept trying to make out the words you were shouting,
but my blood was roaring so loudly in my ear
I thought for sure I had gone deaf.
I tried reading your lips,
but the vertigo was getting
worse with the car going so fast.
I threw up in my mouth a little.
I trailed my hand from your arm to your upper back,
making small circular motions
like when my babies had the colic.

After forever,
you began to slow down

and, gradually, my blood stopped
banging against my eardrums,
and I could make out words, but barely.
Then my ears popped,
like when you're in an airplane
and you chew some gum,
and I heard you shout:

——Don't you know never to argue wid a man
when he's driving? Says so in de fucking driver's manual!

June 21

It is summer solstice
I buried the life we had
to plant a new one.

On the Road to Milk River Bath

I had a dream that I was driving in Jamaica—something I never do.
I was on my way to Milk River Bath in Clarendon Parish.

When I turned off May Pen road—onto the few miles of un-paved track
There it was—stretching out for miles before me like the Savannah.

A sea of green—acres of lush grassland dotted with Acacia trees in flower
Dozens of goats grazed among a handful of sleepy looking Indian cows.

Sun was just setting. Sky catwalked in purples, blues, pinks, and golds
Horizon stretched an open hand, a respite from the mad traffic.

Suddenly a large bird appeared in the sky—dark with the widest wing span
She cast her shadow over the acacia trees, blotting out the waning light.

She cried out to me in a language I almost recognized: Ca-Caw, Ca-Caw!
I strained my ear—as if at any moment I would understand her words.

Then she looked straight at me. For one brief moment our eyes met.
I recognized those eyes. I had seen them somewhere before—but where?

I looked away—she hoisted those majestic wings and flew up, into the sky.
Dark fell like a shroud. A sudden wind troubled the long grass. I shuddered.

I had never felt so alone. I pressed the clutch to the floor, shifted gears.
And gunned the rental towards the healing waters of Milk River.

Smoke in the Acacia Trees

The faint sweet scent of pinewood burning
Smoke rising over the acacia trees
A light wind ruffling the sleeves of morning
My heart broken—wide open
Ready to be filled again.

ACKNOWLEDGMENTS

Sincere thanks to my editor, Christen Kincaid, without whose hard work and dedication this manuscript would not have evolved into the book you're holding in your hands. In recognizing the worth of this collection and agreeing to publish it you have nudged me to turn these poems loose and set them adrift into the big, scary, wonderful world—may they have a rich and layered life. Thanks also to Leah Maines, and everyone at Finishing Line Press who contribute to the success of the press and to the making of this book. Special thanks to the brilliant and acclaimed poets who so generously offered their support by reading this work and writing wonderful blurbs: Denise Duhamel, Honorée Fanonne Jeffers, and Cheryl Boyce Taylor. I also thank my talented son, Jedhi Weir, for the amazing artwork on the cover. To the friends, colleagues, fans and family who preordered this book, thanks for your faith in me and your patience with this process.

My first readers were Melinda Goodman (my first poetry instructor and biggest supporter of my writing), Shelley Tennenbaum, Max Freesney Pierre and Lorraine Stanchich Brown. Your generous praise gave me the boost I needed to complete the work—thanks so much for your kindness. Special thanks also to Andrea Queeley who organized the Writers in Progress Series hosted by AADS at Florida International University in which this work was first discussed publicly, and a big shout out to my readers in the WIP series, Vicki Silvera and Alexandra Cornelius, whose critical insights and warm reception of the work were so important when doubt set in. Andrea, Reyni, and everyone involved in the series thanks for allowing me a safe space to introduce this sensitive work.

Meri-Jane Rochelson, thanks for the support you have always shown to me both professionally and personally, and thanks for your feedback at the WIP reading.

Heather Russell, Pepper Black, Loris Kirkpatrick, Andrea Shaw—so much gratitude for your support of me and my kids. Thanks for being the ride or die sisters I needed in a difficult season. Hang in there with me for sweeter times.

I am grateful for the loving support of current students, alumni and Teaching Assistants from Florida International University who keep me honest and accountable as a writer, teacher and mentor. I will not attempt to name all of you, but you know how special you are to me. Special thanks to Kimberly Gowie, Fabienne Josaphat, Jehanne Gumbs, Tiffany Pogue, and Jheanelle Haynes whose support has been unwavering.

Last, but by no means least, I thank my family— my mother, stepdad, and my three sons whose daily support keeps me going and growing, and my dad, stepmom, sisters, brothers and cousins whose prayers and encouragement keep me strong.

For all of you, just know that there is a lot more I could say, but some things should be said in person. I love and appreciate you all.